LET THE PROPHETS SPEAK

Understanding prophetic ministry

Torrona Tillman & Crystal Jones

Let the Prophets Speak

Understanding Prophetic Ministry

published by

Destiny House Publishing, LLC.

P.O. Box 19774

Detroit, MI 48219

inquiry@destinyhousepublishing.com

www.destinyhousepublishing.com

404.993.0830

Cover by Kingdom Graphic Designs

Printed in the United States

ISBN: 1936867206
ISBN-13: 978-1-936867-20-2

DEDICATIONS

We dedicate this book to all of our spiritual children and to all those who are lovers of truth and seeking Kingdom understanding about the prophetic. May the information in this book arm you with what you need to operate in the prophetic realm and fulfill your Kingdom assignment.

ACKNOWLEDGMENTS

We give all glory to our Outstanding Triune God. Thank you for counting us worthy by putting us into the ministry. We are honored for the calling on our lives as prophets in this end-time hour. We do not take this call lightly. May You be glorified through our efforts to share what we've learned with others. It is certain, we could do none of this without You.

Torrona: To Larry, my husband and my rock, thank you for loving me and taking such great care of our family. I am forever thankful for you allowing me to be me. You are a true expression of His love in my life and I love you always and forever.

To my children, Lauren Renee' and Larry Jr., you are my sunshine and my joy, thanks for loving me back. I love you both to infinity.

To Crystal Jones, my dear friend and spiritual twin, you encouraged me to push past my limits and share what He has shared with me, thank you for being a true expression of God's grace in my life.

To Oscar Jones, my brother, thanks for always being a true friend and a Kingdom gentleman. We appreciate you so much for sharing your treasure with us.

Crystal: To Torrona, the TNT to the enemy. Thank you for being my friend and partner in ministry. I am honored to work with you on this book.

To our amazing husbands, Apostle Oscar Jones and Apostle Larry Tillman, the men who celebrate and cheer us on to do what God has called us to do. We love you and appreciate your leadership in our lives. We could do none of this without your support. Thank you for your confidence in us.

CONTENTS

1

PROPHESY TO THE WIND

"If the church does not recapture its prophetic zeal, it will become an irrelevant social club without moral or spiritual authority." ~Dr. Martin Luther King, Jr.

What a profound statement! And we find ourselves here in this 21st century smack dab in the middle of an amoral society subject to no spiritual authority. How far we've tumbled down the slippery slope! Those words echo in our souls.

Nevertheless our God still sits on the throne. And even though our society is lacking immensely in morals, character, and Christian virtue, our God is still speaking. He still has much to say to those who will hear. Our Amazing God has limited Himself to His unique partnership with mankind.

Surely the Sovereign Lord does nothing without revealing his plan to his servants, the prophets. Amos 3:7

And so though the world lay in waste, He calls for those that would speak on His behalf. Just as He did with Ezekiel. He took Ezekiel to the bleak and barren valley in a vision to show him the state of the church – empty of power and life. The church was totally disconnected and had been in this state for a long time. And then the Lord, our God urged Ezekiel to prophesy. We all know that God could have spoken to those dry bones himself. But he will not violate his own commands. And so He nudges the prophet to step up and speak.

It is the prophetic voice that brings restoration and restructure. God uses men to speak on his behalf. The enemy is strategic in trying to hinder the work of God. He changes laws and times Daniel 7:25 states clearly that the enemy will defy God and attempt to wear out the saints of God. His strategy has been to change the times and laws. And boy has he been busy!! We are still reeling as laws are being changed every day to reflect the degradation of our society. We are getting further and further from the truth. But God says it's only for a time. In the meantime, he appoints men and women to declare his word of promise.

In the vision, we see the Lord, even gives Ezekiel the words to declare. And Ezekiel responds, "I prophesied as I was commanded." He didn't add or take away from what God said. What the Lord said was enough. His word is active and filled with power. The word of the Lord will not return void. Once it is released, it must accomplish that which it was sent to complete. And so the very bones, to which he prophesied, began to shake and move and obey the word of the Lord as released through the prophet. Bones came together. Tendons and flesh came upon the bones. But they still laid lifeless.

And then God said to Ezekiel, "Prophesy to the winds." This is the best part of the text. It is time for fulfillment. The fullness of time has come. And so God shifts Ezekiel. No more prophecy to the bones. It is now time to do something totally out of the ordinary. Wasn't it enough to speak to dead bones? But here comes the boom. Can you imagine? In the natural realm, it seems kind of silly. But when you shift to the spiritual realm, it reveals the power of our God and the authority He grants to us. The wind was an emblem of the Spirit of God, and represented his awakening powers. It created war- like energy when Ezekiel prophesied to the winds.

Speak to the four winds

God wanted Ezekiel to tell them to blow life into the dead. And the winds obeyed Ezekiel. When he looked there was an exceeding great army revived and activated, ready to move as a kingdom people. All of this happened because one man was willing to agree with God and speak what He said to speak. This vision would come to pass.

Our Kind King is full of mercy and love. He looks to this wicked earth with love in His eyes and refuses to leave us in our state of desolation. There is a promise of restoration, reconstruction and reconciliation. And so He summons to Himself a prophetic people to speak and move on His behalf. He needs those who will not only warn, but encourage.

If we are willing to speak for God and see the miraculous, we must first be willing to walk intimately with Him. It's time spent with Him that helps us to distinguish His voice from all other voices, including our own. Note that Ezekiel was an obedient servant of God. He walked very closely to God in his role as priest. He obeyed God without question or hesitation.

We cannot be a people who avoid spending time with God, making excuses of busyness and work. Prophetic people are defined by the time they spend in the presence of God. It is everything. Studying God's word and spending time in prayer is essential to the prophetic. We do not want to taint prophecy. And it is easy to do when we are slow to find ourselves in the presence of God. If we are going to see God's great work accomplished, we must be in proper position. Prophetic people separate themselves from the world and hold fast to the truths of God's word. It is crucial. Then we can prophesy to the wind and see a great revival in the earth.

2

COMMUNICATION WITH GOD

Prayer changes things.

We've heard it a million times before. This statement is so widely used that it comes across as cutesy or cliché-ish. Most hardly even believe it. But the fact of the matter is – prayer really does change life circumstances. We must remember that everything written in scripture takes us back to communication with God

The Old Testament begins in the Garden of Eden with God communicating with Adam, while the New Testament ends with God communicating with John on the Isle of Patmos. From beginning to end everything is hinged on our communication with God. His Spirit goes throughout the earth looking for someone who has established a relationship with Him that He can show himself strong in. II Chronicles 16:9.

In this book, we are directing our attention to prophetic people who have decided that they want to be that 'one' whom Father can show Himself strong in and bring glory to his name. Thus we must all begin with relationship, which begins with repentance; then submission that leads to obedience. We, His prophetic sons and daughters, must come to a place where we value intercession, as something more than an evening service event. Our Father in Heaven requests our total submission and uncompromising obedience. He loved us so much that He gave His best for ours. What a grand start to an amazing journey never to be disregarded or taken lightly. To clearly understand the purpose, we must grasp and hold on to the power of intercession. Intercession is defined by Webster's Dictionary as "to intercede on behalf of another; to strongly urge or petition on behalf of someone else." It is an act of sacrifice that requires a heart to see the best outcome for someone else with no desire for personal gain. Intercession will cost you something.

In today's church, intercession seems to have taken a back row seat, while prosperity, personal fame and success have taken prominence. Intercession flows from the heart of God and the character of Christ. We must pray and transcend into intercession where lives are changed, and souls are saved. Standing in the gap for someone is a privilege and an honor bestowed upon us from the heavens. Our Christian faith is based on intercession; Christ petitioning with His shed blood on behalf of our eternal souls. What an amazing God who loved us before we ever knew Him! We as His intercessors in the earth must also stand for those who have never met us. Intercession is not a focus of prayer for family and friends only. It is a petition submitted on behalf of those Jesus leads us to pray for.

Praying on behalf of another as the Holy Spirit leads is what makes intercession such a powerful weapon in our spiritual arsenal. Our flesh, our personal agenda, is removed from the equation altogether.

We, as His sons and daughters, have committed to do His bidding in the earth. It is our job to pray for whom and what is on Father God's heart. If we are led by our own agenda, or what and whom we think is important, we would surely miss the mark. Scripture encourages us to petition on behalf of all saints and all men (mankind) [Ephesians 6:18 and I Timothy 2:1]. This charge that has been entrusted to us is not only a great responsibility, but an honor as well.

Now that we have touched on the importance of intercession, let's expound on the role that the "prophetic" plays in prayer. We understand that the prophetic stems from the gifting of foretelling or speaking forth. Therefore when we choose to embark upon prophetic intercession, we are submitting to the Holy Spirit to use us in the realm of the spirit to speak forth His will. We are not simply praying and standing in the gap on behalf of someone else, but we have yielded to the Holy Spirit using us to speak in prayer His driving will and purpose. Just as we trust the Spirit of God to use us in prophecy, we must trust Him in prophetic intercession. We as prophetic sons and daughters must have faith to hear in our spirit what will happen, come to pass or manifest.

In training and encouraging young prophets, we let them know that when you do not believe you have a specific word of prophecy from the Holy Spirit for an individual, you always can yield to Holy Spirit for a prophetic prayer. Praying prophetically over an individual will cause you to rest and yield to the Spirit immediately. Father is always speaking, but we are not always listening. Therefore, we trust the Spirit of God to pray through us His divine will in the moment. That is just one aspect of the prophetic intercession and when we learn to rest in His presence He uses us for His glory and His glory alone.

Another aspect of prophetic intercession is praying by His Spirit and speaking forth prophetic declarations over people and places. You may be asking yourself, what in the world do you mean by that? Am I just to stand and declare things I hear in my spirit? Absolutely. Prophets in the office have a further range of authority in the spirit realm than those who operate under the spirit or gift of prophecy. This is why the enemy fights those in the office so hard. He knows that if they ever understood their true power, authority and range in the spirit realm they would bring a completely different level of attack on his plans. This is a war that we know, without a shadow of a doubt, we will win. The problem is we still have to engage in warfare to get to the winning circle. The enemy of our souls knows this, but the everyday Christian and the 'take-it-easy' prophet do not weight its reality heavily. What is a take-it-easy prophet? These are the prophets with the authority, ability, gifting, power and range in the spirit realm to do damage to the enemy, but refuse because it requires too much sacrifice. Prophetic intercession is a powerful weapon in our artillery but without the willingness or training to use it, we lose some battles that we should have won hands down.

Prophetic people can make an impact in the spirit realm for people and places. It requires coming closer to the throne to touch the heart of God. Prophetic people choose to be different, set apart and even misunderstood and rejected to stay in a place where God can have their attention. Therefore, when entering into intercession, we go into realms where few travel because we choose to make the sacrifice to do so. Prophetic intercession is not speaking forth things with a loud voice hoping to gain the ear of a distant god. It is not screaming to the top of our lungs at an enemy that we hope to intimidate. Jesus already won the war; therefore Satan has no power except what we relinquish to him. We are not running into a dark room making noise to scare the boogeyman away. Some prophetic intercessors take that route. It doesn't do anything except keep you busy and make you tired.

When entering in for the purpose of intercession, one thing very helpful is music that stirs the soul. Music is a conduit that can take you in and out of zones. The world uses music on a regular basis to control atmospheres. Whether it is shopping, partying, or eating. Even if you watch movies you will notice that the musical score is a major key in the success of that movie. So much so, that there are awards for the music composers. We will discuss that further in a later chapter. The proper music in prophetic intercession truly shifts the atmosphere for the move and leading of the Holy Spirit.

The study of the word of God is another major component to intercession. Many prophetic people slack when it comes to studying the Word. However the effective intercessor does not give themselves that option. The Bible says in

John 1:14 "And the Word was made flesh and dwelt among us, (and we beheld his glory, the glory as of the only begotten of the Father), full of grace and truth." Jesus is the Word made flesh.

He is the Word and the Word is His will. To know the will, the ways and the heart of God, we must know His Word. To pray outside of that knowledge will lead you into prayers full of emotions and self-centeredness. We pray according to our hearts and minds and opposed to His. The study and knowledge of His Word is not an option. It is a necessity. We prophesy by His Spirit, but His Spirit and His Word are one and cannot be separated. I say what He says, and I pray what is in His heart, therefore I must be a student of His Word to know His mind and heart. Prophetic intercessors must know the Word of God to pray by His Spirit. Father, Son, and Holy Spirit, they are one.

Prophetic intercession is a strategy released from Heaven's boardroom that will put our enemy to flight and even cancel out his assignments on the earth. Before engaging, there are questions that must be asked and answered. Questions such as, "What am I praying for? Who am I praying for? What outcome am I releasing? Which direction am I headed in the spirit realm? Who and what must I shut down in order for God's army to penetrate the region? Is this my region and assignment? And what time constraints am I working under?" Those are just a few of the questions that we as prophetic strategists must answer when we enter into prophetic intercession. You have to pray with purpose and strategy, or you will repeatedly be hitting and missing with no success or victory.

Wildly hitting and missing is usually followed by discouragement and too much downtime due to that discouragement. A lot of Christian soldiers are in recovery from a battle they have not even fought. They only think they have because of spiritual discouragement cloaking itself as wounds from the enemy. They back up or take down for a season. Then the church comes along and labels them wounded soldiers, and they are allowed to stay off the battlefield until they heal. I am definitely not insinuating that the army of God doesn't have wounded soldiers, for surely we do. What I am saying is that when we have more wounded warriors than we do soldiers on the battlefield.

That is the deceiver at work. He has worked on the hearts and minds of God's people so tough that we don't recognize fear and disappointment for what it is. We take soldiers out of prayer and intercession and put them in the spiritual hospitals; while in the spirit realm the kingdom and the earth are left with more unprotected territories.

Prophetic intercession is intercession from trained and armed soldiers who have learned to wage war against the enemy and continue watch over territories that have already been taken. Prophetic intercession is never to be reduced to a weekly event in our churches. It is a routine part of our life as soldiers in the army of the Lord. The enemy hits, and he can hit hard. Yet we continue to stand and fight. Soldiers understand that they are fighting for the man next to them and for a people, nation and cause bigger than they are. Therein is the power of intercession. Standing in the gap for someone else with no consideration of personal gain, loss or acknowledgement.

We intercede as a prophetic people the way Elijah interceded for Israel in I Kings the 17th and 18th chapters. We read how Father God had Elijah to declare the heavens be shut, and how he had Elijah declare the heavens be opened, three years later. If you are unfamiliar with the details of this awesome move of God, please read the chapters stated above.

In a time, where it seemed as though all was lost for Israel, God sent a prophetic intercessor to stand in the gap for a people and place with no promise of personal gain. During this drought that Father had released on the earth, He made provision for his prophet but there were no promises of wealth or fame. True prophets teach wealth and provision for the benefit of blessing citizens of the Kingdom of God. Father God releases wealth in His kingdom to keep the storehouses full. Only then can we extend His kingdom by reaching souls as He adds to the church daily. We should never teach prosperity for selfish gain. We as his servants, may accumulate wealth on our journey or we may not, but to the true prophet and prophetic people contentment is great gain.

Elijah the prophet and servant of the LORD, stood in the gap for Israel and made great sacrifices to do so. Even though we read that he won the battle on Mt. Carmel (I Kings 18:16-39), the mental and emotional strain of Jezebel's threats and intimidation were too much for him to handle. In this account, we must understand that Elijah was not a prophet who turned cowardly and ran from Jezebel, a murderess of prophets. He was a soldier who had just come out of a serious battle in which he and his God won. He was so drained that he didn't realize that the same God that made a spectacle of the false prophets on Mt. Carmel was well able to cancel every threat Jezebel unleashed on him. This is such a real display of warfare and intercession in the body of Christ today.

Warfare wins victories for the masses, but drains and weakens the warrior. In the time of weakness, when the warrior should retreat for a refreshing, they can make decisions that will negatively impact their lives and those around them. What do we think the other prophets thought about Elijah taking flight from the intimidation of Jezebel? Did his flight from Jezebel challenge Israel's faith in God? What we do always affects those around us, therefore let's weigh our decisions with that in mind. We must always remember that we are part of an army of warriors. We are never to be a one-man crew, even though we are the person in the forefront. It would have been best for all if Elijah had walked away to rest instead of ran away to hide.

Intercession is the tool Elijah used to defeat the enemy in that warfare for Israel. He first knew the assignment. Secondly, he set the terms of the strategy. Thirdly, he maintained his confidence. Finally, he prayed a powerful prophetic prayer as he stepped back and watched Father remind everyone present that He was the only true and living God.

Victory on Mt Carmel was a victory for Israel; not for Elijah. Prophets make sacrifices while captives are set free, and victories are won throughout the earth. When we as His prophetic people in the earth, taint His glory and power flowing through us with pride and selfish ambitions, strategies are compromised, and battles are lost. We, His prophetic sons and daughters, have power in the heavens and authority in the earth to battle for the souls of men as His Kingdom is established. Prophetic intercession, if engaged righteously and strategically, can change lives and nations for the glory of God. Let us war a good warfare.

3

WE CAN ALL PROPHESY

Follow the way of love and eagerly desire gifts of the Spirit,
especially prophecy. I Corinthians 14:1

Paul encourages us to *desire* the gift of prophecy. In fact, he continues down to the 31st verse and says,

"For you can all prophesy in turn so that everyone may be instructed and encouraged (NIV)."

It is quite exciting to know that we all can prophesy. However understand that does not mean that all believers are prophets or that all have the gift of prophecy. It's quite the contrary.

There are generally 3 levels of prophetic ministry. The first level is for every believer filled with the Holy Ghost. This is what the Bible refers to in Acts the 2nd chapter. That's the level we will be discussing in this chapter. Level 2 is the 'gift' of prophecy. The third level is the 'office' of the prophet. The gift and the office will be discussed in subsequent chapters.

Every believer has the unique privilege and honor of an intimate relationship with God through the Holy Spirit. We can hear God for ourselves, and we can hear His word for others. It flows all out of our time spent in His presence. We can only expect to hear God if we have spent time with Him. The more we take time to develop our personal relationship with God, the better we will be able to hear. We have to be able to discern the voice of God from that of the enemy, and even from our own voice. The only way to recognize someone's voice is to spend time with them. There is no way around it. As we pray and study God's word, we will become more and more consistent in determining what is from God and what is not. Heaven yearns to speak to earth. There is much that the Lord has to say. And He uses people to get his message across. Prophecy is speaking what we hear Him saying. We are simply conduits. We say what He says without addition or subtraction. We release the word in faith.

God's instructions and encouragement is important. And He wants us all to partake both in giving and receiving. As the days grow more evil, we will need to hear from God like never before. We are believing God for a great outpouring of the prophetic. We believe this outpouring is coming as a demonstration of God's grace in the midst of sin and corruption in the earth. It's the grace of God that leads men to repentance. God's grace will be poured out on seniors and children, men and women alike.

This will require 3 elements: faith that works by love, a healthy knowledge of the word of God, and practice.

Romans 12:6 Having gifts that differ according to the grace given to us, let us use them: if prophecy, in proportion to our faith.

16

We are to prophesy according to the proportion of our faith. You can have faith to prophesy to 1 person or 1,000. As we continue to hear God's word in this area we can grow in our faith.

Often we do not release the prophetic utterance, even though we may have a strong impression that we hear God speaking. Our hindrances are often due to fear. The enemy seeks to wrap us up in fear so that we will disobey the instructions of God. He taunts us with, "What if you are wrong?" You sweat, your heart starts beating rapidly, your mouth gets dry. But what if you are wrong? Please know, that the earth will not open up and swallow you. You will learn, develop and continue to mature.

We are all human and subject to err. God doesn't punish us when we fail. There is grace enough for us to grow. Consider what the focus is. It starts out as God's Word to the receiver. But the enemy injects fear into the equation and moves the focus to the giver of the word. Shifty! We are no longer concerned about the other person but now we are more interested in ourselves - being right.

When you hear the enemy speak the loudest, "What if you are wrong?" those are generally the times that God is speaking. And the enemy doesn't want you to deliver the word. This is not true every single time. But it is generally a good indicator.

God's word is usually meant to bless both the giver and the receiver. This is where faith and practice comes in. You just do it. Take the risk. Get it out. And the more we do, the stronger we become. Carefully phrase the word, "I think God is saying..." "I believe the Lord wants me to tell you..." It's even okay to say, "I'm not sure but this is what I sense God saying…" This will squash the voice of the enemy in your ear. You are acknowledging your humanness as you deliver a divine word. This also keeps us in a place of humility.

Another weapon of fear is "What if the message isn't received?" Again the focus is on us and not the intended. That one is a little more obvious. We are not responsible for whether someone receives the word. We are only accountable for delivering it. You are simply a mailman. So anyone you deliver a message to has the right to reject it. They can write on the envelope – return to sender. Your assignment is simply the delivery. The rest is between them and God.

We can never think that we are always 100% on target with our words. And that everyone must take heed and obey us. It can cause us to become puffed up, thinking more of ourselves than we ought. We should *expect* a word to be examined.

When we speak to the body of Christ as a prophetic people or a person operating with a gift of prophecy, we generally speak words that strengthen, encourage, and comfort. The goal of the gift is to bring out the best in others.

But the one who prophesies speaks to people for their strengthening, encouraging and comfort. I Corinthians 14:3 NIV

God speaks to us in different expressions. The following is a list of the various ways we are able to hear God's message.

Ministering in the Prophetic:

The Bible – The Holy Spirit is able to bring scripture passages to our minds. This is the foundation of prophecy. Prophecy must never contradict the Word of God.

His Voice – You can hear God speak to you. It is not necessarily an audible voice, but definitely there is an impression of words in your mind.

The Imagination – There are pictures, or symbols that you can see in your mind.

The Emotions – We can pick up on others' emotions. Or we can feel anger, anxiousness, heaviness, etc.

Physical – God speaks to us by letting us feel physical sensations maybe a pain, warmth, or tingling.

There are other ways that God speaks: angels, music, nature, dreams, visions, trances, etc.

We will all hear God's voice in more than one way. So do not limit him to your dreams or any other expression. He wants us to press into him. He wants to be discovered. So there will be seasons where he will deal with you in one particular way and then He will change it to summon us closer to Himself. This causes us to go deeper in our seek. We don't want to get comfortable or stuck in one expression. God retains the right to be Himself and speak however He chooses.

4

THE GIFT

In my journey with the Lord, I (Prophetess Tillman) have seen and heard a lot on and about prophecy and the prophetic. One of the most challenging and controversial subjects in the body of Christ is the subject of the prophetic. There are those who say the gift is not for today, there are those who say it is only for an elite group, and there are even those who say, 'I don't want it operating in my church.' We know that as a multitude of believers that stretch across the globe, we are not going to always agree on everything. With this understanding may I encourage you to read this chapter carefully along with your Bible. I will not attempt to go into deep waters where you will need to put on your deep-sea diving gear, but I will attempt to enlighten you enough where you can swim with confidence.

Over the years, I have never attempted to write anything concerning the prophetic ministry. There was always this thought that enough was already being said. Well, because of a very special friend, Crystal Jones, prophetess of God, publisher of Destiny House Publishing, and co-author of this book, that way of thinking has come to an end. I agree that we all have a unique voice to speak to a unique people and because of that I am now speaking to you. "Hello, unique one!"

In the body of Christ, we all have been given gifts and assignments from the throne room of God. Each and every one of us, has been created with purpose and destiny secretly coded in our DNA. I use the words 'secretly coded' because if it weren't, the enemy of our souls would have easy access. The other good thing about our destiny code being secret, is that even we don't have the access code, only the Holy Spirit. When we are living our lives outside the will of God and doing everything we are big enough to do, I do not believe Father gives us full access to our true gifting. We would probably mishandle, squander and even sell our birthright, at first opportunity. We may experience some benefits that lead us or others to believe that there is something different about us, but full access isn't granted until our will is surrendered to Christ. In all wisdom, Father God always seems to hide treasures until an appointed time, for the good of all.

The prophetic ministry is one such gifting that truly requires an access code. It is not designed to be picked up off the shelf in a mega supermarket or obtained online for a lesser price. This anointing is costly. It is so costly and rare that you won't find a coupon or discount code anywhere. Unfortunately, some of the happenings among the prophetic people of God makes me wonder if someone isn't manufacturing coupons and passing them around to folk. Even if you have come across a few coupons or discount codes, may I encourage you to destroy any and all of those in your possession. This is not that type of party.

The ministry of prophecy is for those who have been called away from the hustle and bustle of carnality, even in the Kingdom, and set apart to declare His Words and His Heart in the earth. With that kind of assignment we can't afford to be entangled with the affairs of this life. Now don't get me wrong, you should keep your job, stay married, love and raise your children, enjoy your friendships, vote in the next election, go roller skating, take long walks and enjoy the best this world has to offer. What I am referring to is getting so wrapped up in the system of this world that we fail to stay in the presence of our God. In His presence is the only place to hear His voice that we may speak His words and proclaim His will in the earth.

The two areas of prophetic ministry that I would like to discuss in this chapter are the spirit of prophecy and the gift of prophecy.

The office of the prophet will be discussed in a separate chapter. The spirit of prophecy is what I would term a grace freely given to every born-again Christian. The Bible says in I Corinthians 14:1-3, Follow after charity and desire spiritual gifts, but rather that ye may prophesy. For he that speaketh in an unknown tongue speaketh not unto men, but unto God: for no man understandeth him; howbeit in the spirit he speaketh mysteries. But he that prophesieth speaketh unto men to edification, and exhortation, and comfort."

Many times this anointing is stirred in an atmosphere of worship and faith. The wonderful thing about the God we serve is He truly is a God of order. It is His signature in all He does. Even when it seems the spirit is flowing freely, there is order to the flow. In the house of God with clear order and oversight is the best atmosphere for the spirit of prophecy to flow and maintain that order. God will usually shift the atmosphere in the service, through ordained leadership, for the flow of Holy Spirit in prophecy. This does not mean during worship you tap your neighbor on the shoulder and give him or her a 'word from the Lord'. The spirit of prophecy being stirred in an atmosphere of worship and faith can take place at church, at prayer or in the family room, but it is best in the presence of mature spiritual believers or leaders. I don't believe Holy Spirit just pops in while we are watching our favorite family show and begins speaking through someone. Neither does He prefer to stop you coming out of the bathroom and throw a word at you. He doesn't want His Voice to become so casual that we lose reverence for His Presence.

Praying in the spirit, reading our Bibles, studying the scriptures, living holy, places us in a position for the Holy Spirit to freely flow by faith through us. It is not considered works or perfection, but preparation with expectancy. Can a novice and newly born-again Christian prophesy? Of course. The spirit of prophecy is the testimony of Christ according to Revelation 19:10. Just like salvation, it is open to all those who receive it by faith.

Paul, according to I Corinthians 14:1-5, says he that prophesies edifies or builds up the church. The commitment to prayer and the Word of God simply places a believer in a position to hear more clearly what Holy Spirit is speaking to him. It is like having a dull knife that barely cuts and a sharpened knife that slices without resistance. We are tools or instruments for Holy Spirit to use in the earth for the glory of God. I am confident that because you are reading this book, you are a son or daughter who desires to be used by Father with all your heart. May I encourage you to seek to prophesy by faith, trusting Holy Spirit to flow through you freely as He wills.

Now let's talk about the gift of prophecy. The gift of prophecy unlike the spirit of prophecy has two major components we must discuss. One is frequency and the other is range. First, let's talk of frequency. When I say frequency, I am referring to how often the spirit of prophecy flows through an individual. Unlike the general flow of the spirit of prophecy, the gift of prophecy flows much more frequently producing a greater confidence through reason of use of the gift. The frequency of prophecy for those with the gift is limitless.

With the gift, you may speak a word at lunch with a friend, share with someone on the plane, leave a message by unction of Holy Spirit on a voicemail. This does not mean I am contradicting myself. Above, I stated that Holy Spirit maintains His reverence and order at all times, this remains true. When you believe you have a word from the Lord, a servant flowing in the gift should ask the person they desire to share with, if it is ok that they release what they hear in the spirit. Remember the spirit and gift do not have the same authority as the office. Therefore, in humility and wisdom we ask, then boldly proclaim. Lunching with a friend, Holy Spirit, may impress upon someone with the gift to ask the other person if they can speak what they hear in their spirit. This will probably not be a word about world peace. Normally this will be a word for the person sitting right in front of the vessel speaking. Order and timing are key factors here. Order, because he or she asked if they can share, and timing because they are in agreement in that moment about what God has to say. The person receiving can and should judge the prophecy as to whether it is valid. Usually, the receiver will immediately know that it is Father speaking to them because it agrees with their spirit, lines up with scripture and touches on something Father God has been dealing with them about. Even leaving a voice message, the person who will hear the prophecy has the opportunity to receive or reject the message. I personally suggest you don't leave voice messages, unless absolutely necessary, but be patient and request the person call you back.

The gift of prophecy is listed in I Corinthians 12:10 and Romans 12:6, please be sure to read the complete chapters for contextual understanding and clarity. All gifts have been predetermined since the beginning of time and are given by God and Him alone. I cannot decide that through prayer and consecration that I want to operate in the gift of prophecy, but I can yield myself to Holy Spirit to use me in that gift if it has already been encoded in my DNA. The gift of prophecy, like the spirit of prophecy, is for edification, exhortation and comfort. It doesn't come with the authority to govern, rebuke, or correct. That comes with the office of the prophet which is discussed in the next chapter.

The second component I would like to talk about is range. When I say range, I am referring to whom we prophesy to and how deep it goes. Those who flow in the gift have a greater range than those who can prophesy by the unction of Holy Spirit at particular times. I may be able to minister a word from the Lord on a street corner to an individual, but that does not mean I have the gift of prophecy. It means I have learned to tune in to the prophetic grace that God has given to all believers. We can all prophesy, but we do not all have the gift or operate in the office of the prophet. It is imperative that I share that as we continue in our discussion of this particular gift. The range means that I can flow confidently, freely, frequently and accurately anywhere at any time. Even the content of what is released from Holy Spirit is broader in range. Holy Spirit through the gift of prophecy can impress upon you to share the month a woman will conceive a child, the sex of the child and how many children the woman already has. In the church today, if a person can prophesy that kind of word, someone is about to call them and set a date for their ordination into the office. That is a dangerous move. Just like frequency and range can be used to determine the gift of prophecy, it should also 'not' be used to determine that the person should be in the office of a prophet.

There are so many believers in the body of Christ who operate in the gift of prophecy, and because of frequency and range believe they are automatically in the office. This deception will cause a prophetic person to step out of their grace, which leads to attacks that they are not able to handle or overcome. The attack of Satan on every believer is real and should be expected. There are no exemptions to this warfare. The key is that we are graced by God to handle and withstand attacks when operating in our grace. If I prophesy a few times accurately in church, it does not mean I operate in the gift of prophecy. If I prophesy frequently outside the church it does mean I operate in the office of the prophet.

The gift of prophecy not only has a great frequency and range, but the dynamics of operation are great as well. With this gift, a person can travel around the world in prophetic teams and prophesy to nations. Dreaming is a part of that gifting. Prophetic song is a dynamic of that gifting, prophetic dance is a part of that gifting, prophetic writing is as well. With the gift of prophecy there are no limitations as to how Holy Spirit can use you. Remember, you are unique. Even with all of these dynamics and variations of the gift, don't allow the enemy of your soul or people within your circle to push you out of the will of

God. There are hearts that need to hear your voice and the words in your mouth are for the nations. May I encourage you to seek His face and flow by His Spirit and His Spirit alone.

Prophetic people are unique individuals and sometimes find it difficult to fit into the everyday flow of the church and the world system. They are people of prayer and intercession, and often times seem strange to those who don't understand the gift. I have heard more times than I can count from those who flow in this gift that they thought they were crazy or were losing their minds. Many times this is because they are in a spiritual drought from lack of affirmation, teaching, and training.

Prophetic atmospheres that minister to the spirit of a prophetic person are as essential as water and sunshine are to flowers, lawns, or gardens. This does not mean you have to leave your church, but it does mean you may not feel comfortable in every church or ministry. Attend a school of the prophets, with a seasoned prophet you can trust, for affirmation and instruction. If God leads you, ask your senior leader if he or she would consider hosting a school of the prophets. It will change your life and bless the ministry beyond words. I pray that in reading this chapter, your knowledge has increased, and your confidence strengthened as you walk out your prophetic journey or encourage someone else on theirs.

5

THE OFFICE OF THE PROPHET AND OTHER GOVERNMENTAL OFFICES

Let the prophet speak!

To proclaim this in the earth is groundbreaking and truly life changing. When the prophet speaks all of heaven backs him or her up, and all of hell trembles. How can I say this so confidently? Because I understand the office and the impact that Father God intended this office to hold. If I lacked that knowledge I would second guess or hesitate to speak boldly 'what thus saith the Lord'. Walking in this office is no-joke and no-cakewalk. Walking in any five-fold ministry office is no easy task. Therefore I must encourage you to listen with your spirit for the sound of heaven. In reading this chapter, if you operate in the office of the prophet, you will begin to hear a distinct sound resonating through your spirit shifting things around. There will be a connection that will alter your thinking, refresh your spirit, and restore your soul. There is always a sound before a change. Yes and Amen.

I was called to the office of a prophet before my mother conceived me in her womb. This was the confidence Jeremiah walked in after he embraced the word from God spoken to him in Jeremiah 1:5, "Before I formed thee in the belly I knew thee; and before thou camest forth out of the womb I sanctified thee, and I ordained thee a prophet to the nations." The office of the prophet is not one chosen by man; but God. Whether it is words or dreams, you begin to notice that there is something different. Father called Jeremiah to be a prophet to the nation, Israel. He had to overcome his fears, doubts and shortcomings in order to receive 'what thus saith the Lord.' I am reflecting on this text because it is the route of every prophet receiving the call to this office. We don't run to it, happen upon it or demand it. We just live life and then stuff starts happening. All kinds of stuff.

The office of the prophet is like none of the other five-fold ministry offices found in Ephesians 4:7-12, but I do personally consider it to be the companion of the apostle. The Bible says in Ephesians 2:20 the foundation of the church is built on the apostles and prophets with Jesus being the chief cornerstone. The establishing and directional graces of these offices is what we all stand on. These two gifts work so closely together that some find it hard to separate them in their vocabulary. Paul, the Apostle says in I Corinthians 12:28 that God set some in the church, first apostles, secondarily prophets. This order should not be understood in terms of hierarchy or importance, but rather a divine order of function. Within every family, the birth number of the children have significance. This truth applies to the first and second of the five-fold, the apostle and the prophet. The apostle being the first born, and then the prophet. If we take note, many times the first and second siblings of a group of five or more may be closer to each other than the other siblings. I believe we can see this more times than not in a typical family. The first and second child experience such a different family dynamic than the others. They are at the top of the gene pool, they have been with mom and dad the longest, and the first born met and established a relationship with the second born, before any of the others that followed. Now we can see why the titles, 'apostle and prophet' roll off the tongues of God's people so easily. Let's move forward for some more understanding.

The book of Ephesians was written by the Apostle Paul to the church at Ephesus. This is not known to be a book addressing specific troubles in the church, but one full of revelation and exhortation. In the fourth chapter, Paul shares his revelation of Jesus Christ. He states that when Jesus ascended He gave gifts to men, not men in gender, but mankind. According to Strong's Concordance, the word men by definition in the Greek (reference 444- anthropos) refers to male or female, human race. This is important because most times when we see the word men in the Bible we immediately believe it is referring to a man of male gender only, and therefore that places women in a position of taking something given only to men. This is just not true. Women throughout the Bible operated in gifts and callings that set foundation, gave direction, and established ministries. Whether male or female, Father chooses to use yielded vessels. There is a requirement of love, honor, respect and submission to the gift (not the gender). We are to submit one to another as we reverence and serve our King. With all of our getting, we must get an understanding of scripture and the heart of Father.

The 'office' of the prophet is not synonymous to the gift of prophecy. The gift of prophecy operates in a dimension greater than the spirit of prophecy, and the office of the prophet operates in a dimension greater than the gift. Although, quite like the gift of prophecy, those in the office have a frequency and range that is limitless. The two major components of this office that I would like to address in this chapter is authority and government. These two character traits of those who operate in this office distinctly sets them apart from those who operate in the gift. As I stated in the chapter on prophetic ministry, there is a lot of misunderstanding about these callings that can cause disorder in the body of Christ.

Most people can clearly see that those in the office of the prophet have a particular type of personality that goes along with the calling. It is that of uncanny confidence and authority that can only be given by heaven. Both of these traits have to be developed in the prophet as they walk there journey with the Lord. We must understand that there are those who have authority that don't possess confidence and those with confidence who have no authority. That was a mouthful. I always reference Barney Fife in the old classic television show *Andy Griffith*. For those who aren't familiar, this show was about the life and happenings of a kindhearted and wise sheriff in a small town named Mayberry. In this show, the sheriff's deputy was named Barney Fife. Barney was authorized as deputy, but if you were a regular viewer you were well aware of the fact that he had very little, if any, confidence. He had a badge, a gun and one bullet kept in his uniform shirt pocket. This view of confidence and authority has helped me so much on my journey. Deputy Fife, could only execute his office because he was sworn in by the sheriff and for no other reason. He had authority, but no confidence. Without that badge, he faked confidence every step of the way. There was another character in the show that had confidence and no authority, Ernest T. Bass. He was the town nuisance. He received a uniform once but was not sanctioned. On one episode, he wanted to arrest somebody because they had *done wrong* but he had no authority. These behavior patterns are seen quite often in the body of Christ. Those with the gift rebuking leaders and those in the office refusing to pull that one bullet out of their shirt pocket.

That doesn't mean that because a prophetic person develops confidence he is automatically a prophet. It simply means that you cannot separate the two traits and be a prophet. The most uncertain time in a prophet's life is in becoming aware of the truth that he or she actually walks under that mantle. The realization of that truth can be so overwhelming that it knocks you off your feet. One day, you are serving and loving God, then another day, somewhere down the line of course, you find someone anointing you to the office of a prophet. Even if you have never had hands laid on you, you have had a moment of enlightenment that is quite overwhelming.

Authority is defined by Miriam-Webster Dictionary as 'the power to give orders or make decisions'. Now we understand why prophets are sometimes considered bossy people. I know, it is so hard to imagine. In a truth, that part of their character is one of their distinguishing traits. Actually, it is the distinguishing trait of anyone who walks in a five-fold ministry office. The proper term is not bossiness, but authority. We must remember that each of the five-fold ministry offices listed in Ephesians 4 gifts were given by Jesus Christ. They represent Christ and His authority in His church.

The scripture in Ephesian 4:11 says that "...and he gave some..." The gifts are given. The great question is who can attempt to take credit for something that was given to them? The answer, a false prophet. The Bible, according to Jeremiah 23:21 records Jehovah God saying, "I have not sent these prophets, yet they ran: I have not spoken to them, yet they prophesied." This passage is speaking of false prophets, and notes their fleshly pride and arrogance. If they are bold enough to go and to speak outside of His will, they are foolish enough to attempt to steal His Glory. A true prophet must walk in the authority of the office given him, but He must never allow pride to come in and cause him to take glory or credit due the Lord our God.

Let's restate a previous observation we shared, there are those who have authority that don't possess confidence and those with confidence who have no authority. Let's unpack this a little more. Those with the gift of prophecy speak what 'thus saith the Lord' boldly and confidently by the leading of Holy Spirit. Without the weight of the office resting on their lives, they should not try to execute correction, rebuke, or direction. Crossing that line is a dangerous step. Dangerous meaning that without the power and authority of the office, we can open ourselves up to attacks that can cause permanent or temporary damage to ourselves or the ones who are receiving prophecy. With every gift, is the grace to withstand the attacks of the enemy. Where Father guides, He provides, and that provision includes protection. If we send ourselves, as false prophets do, we are sure to get bulldozed. May I encourage you to walk only in the gift and calling that Father has encoded into your DNA. Many prophetic people open themselves up to attack and to the spirit of Jezebel by attempting to tread where they have no authority.

Confidence and authority in a true prophet sets captives free and prospers all those who believe. I have witnessed those with prophetic graces crash and burn because of their attempt to operate under the mantle of a prophet. With a false sense of confidence and under non-delegated authority, they walk right out of the will of God. When we attempt to operate in an office or under a grace not given by God, we open ourselves up to the influence of ungodly spirits. The spirit of pride, envy and jealousy is always operating in an individual who chooses to covet another person's gift or calling. These are always open doors among prophetic people for the Jezebel spirit to enter. Since jealousy and envy are character traits of the spirit of Jezebel, and her mission is to always silence prophetic voices, we cause a warfare that should never have been waged.

In the days of Elijah, the prophet, Jezebel attempted to destroy the prophets of God because of envy and pride (I Kings 18). She operated under false authority taken from her husband, King Ahab, which simply fed her spirit of pride and eventually caused her demise. That is sure to be the end result for anyone operating as a non-delegated authority. In order to stay in her position, she attempted to rid Israel of the prophets of God, the delegated voices of authority in Israel. In doing so, she believed that the prophets of her false gods would be the only voices Israel would hear. Unfortunately for her, there were seven thousand prophets of God who had not bowed their knee to the false gods of Baal and Asherah. Even though it seems as though the unrighteous are speaking loudly, we must remember that the enemy can never silence the voice of the only true and living God. His prophets will speak and His name will be glorified.

In understanding the office of the prophet in the Kingdom of God, we must hold a brief discussion about governmental order.

According to Merriam Webster Dictionary, Government means political direction and control exercised over the actions of the members, citizens, or inhabitants of communities, societies, and state. Government is absolutely necessary in any society. In the Kingdom of God where Jesus Christ governs, there is always order. I believe that the five-fold ministry represents the hand of Christ and the governing board of the church. As we stated earlier, according to Ephesians 4, Jesus gave gifts unto men. He took of His spirit and released His authority upon the five-fold gifts for the edification of His body. On that governing board, is the apostle, the prophet, the evangelist, the pastor and the teacher. If we as citizens of His Kingdom, in honoring our King, give honor to those who operate under these gifts and mantles, we will experience true and lasting victories.

Let me share a few more thoughts as I close out this chapter. The presence of God is the only place a prophet can hear the voice of God. So without the anointing and commitment to prayer and intercession, a prophet will easily slip out of God's will into His own. Years ago, as I began to pursue the call of the prophet upon my life, I made a call to a prominent ministry for materials on the prophetic.

The gracious administrator that answered my call was a prophet in the house who had just got hired as secretary, which positioned her to answer my call. She, being led by His Spirit, began to share with me wisdom on the call of the prophet. In our brief time on the phone, she asked me numerous questions. One question was, where was I currently serving in ministry? In sharing the areas of ministry I served in, I made mention that I was leader of the intercessory prayer team. She quickly said that was what she was listening for. Her point was that a prophet has to be a person of prayer and order.

After answering that question, she kindly gave me a little spiritual wisdom. She stated that if I am ever in prayer on my face before God, and I open my eyes and see disorder under my bed, I was to get up, clean up and then return to prayer. First of all, disorder is truly my enemy. Secondly, her point was well taken. She shared with me that if you do not know how to maintain order in your own home, how would God dare use you to maintain order in the house of God. The journey to being confirmed as a prophet can take many turns, but by His grace you will find yourself on the road He has ordained for you. That entire conversation years ago with that unknown prophet was life altering for this now seasoned prophet still seeking to walk out His will for her life.

Finally, in the office of the prophet, there will be times where you will need to teach direction, as well as give it. With the prophetic gifting, there will be seasons and times you must step out of the rhema (His spoken word) into the logos (the written Word). Many prophets stay in the rhema too often and become slack in their study and teaching of the written Word of God. It is imperative that we understand the logos and the rhema should co-exist in the heart of a prophet. It doesn't matter whether you operate in the office or the gift. When we prophesy, we do so under authority, and all that we speak forth must line up with the written word. How can we speak a prophetic word without being students and teachers of the written word? It is the written word and the hearing of it that feeds our spirit. In my walk with God, I have found that prophets are spiritually drawn to teachers in the body of Christ. This simply means that a prophet loves the teaching of the word of God. It brings a refreshment to their spirits and healing to their souls. May I encourage you to stay in His presence, stay in His word and stay in His will.

6

DREAMS & VISIONS

"In the last days, God says I will pour out my spirit on all people. Your sons and daughters will prophesy, your young men will see visions, your old men shall dream dreams." Acts 2:17

Some question whether God still gives us dreams and visions today. This Acts passage clearly tells us that *'in the last days'*... I think that is relevant. Those 4 words gives us the confidence that the Lord is still ministering to us today in dreams and visions. And He gives those messages to believers and unbelievers alike.

Dreams are messages communicated to us while we are asleep.

Visions are communicated to us while we are awake. More people are likely to experience dreams than visions. A vision can be influenced by your own thoughts and feelings while dreams tend to be out of our control. But caution: all dreams and visions are NOT from God. Some dreams come from the enemy. Some come from your own cares or worries.

A dream comes when there are many cares, and many words mark the speech of a fool. Ecclesiastes 5:3

You can be so concerned about an issue until you actually dream about it. So we are wise to seek understanding regarding our dreams and visions. One thing is important to remember, God wants you to understand His message to you. He does not give us dreams for amusement or entertainment or as a substitute for relying upon Him and His Word. He wants you to press in and draw closer. Every God-given dream has purpose.

"For God does speak—now one way, now another— though no one perceives it.

[15] In a dream, in a vision of the night, when deep sleep falls on people as they slumber in their beds,

[16] he may speak in their ears and terrify them with warnings,

[17] to turn them from wrongdoing and keep them from pride,

[18] to preserve them from the pit, their lives from perishing by the sword. Job 33:14-18"

According to this passage in Job, dreams and visions have divine purpose. They are given by God to warn us, and to keep us from pride, sin, and snares. So we really need to give more value to them then we do. God is speaking and He wants us to heed His message. We aren't to take it lightly when we have a dream that we believe is God-given.

Dreams and visions can be literal or highly symbolic. If you move too quickly to decipher them, you could easily misinterpret the message. That's why it is so important that we record all of our dreams and visions. Write them down along with the date and time. And allow proper time to discern from God the true revelation.

There are many books that offer an interpretation for words and symbols in your dreams. These are poor tools for understanding what God is saying to you personally. There is no formula for interpreting dreams. God knows His children. He is God to a diverse people who speak and understand different languages. When we attempt to define a symbol as always meaning one thing, no matter who dreams it, we limit God and taint the message. Consider the extreme diversity in our languages. For example, our American term crackers in Australia means Bon Bons. Pillar box in England is a mailbox in the U.S. Different words mean different things. In addition to that, we are all different and have our own unique experiences. So it would do us a great disservice to use a book to discern words and symbols from Heaven.

One 'dream' book says one thing, and another says something else. For example, one book says if you dream about cows, it means you are passive. It indicates your need to belong. Another book says a dream about a cow means something is going to happen to your mother. However when Joseph interpreted Pharoah's dream about cows, they represented years. Fat cows represented years of plenty and lean cows represented years of famine (Genesis 41). Our God is sovereign. He reserves the right to speak to us as He sees fit. We cannot box Him in. The very best interpreter of a dream is the Holy Spirit. So if you have those dream books, toss them away and lean on the Holy Spirit.

Dreams should always be recorded immediately. If we trust our memories, we are sure to forget important details. If you were to awaken in the middle of the night, write down your dream. Write what you saw. Don't judge it. Just write it down. In the same way, visions should be recorded but only after they are complete. Describe them before trying to interpret them. We need to discern if the dreams/visions are messages to us from God.

He said, "Listen to my words: When there is a prophet among you, I, the Lord, reveal myself to them in visions, I speak to them in dreams." Numbers 12:6

Our God uses dreams to disclose His true prophets. If a man or woman of God says that they have received a dream or vision, then *others* will know *they* are a prophet from the Lord. Does that mean that if we have a dream from God then we are automatically deemed prophets? Of course, not. Because as we said before even unbelievers have had dreams from God. In Judges 7:13-14, One man had a dream and the other interpreted it. Both men were the enemies of Israel and God. When Gideon came, behold a man was relating a dream to his friend.

And he said, "behold, I had a dream; a loaf of barley bread was tumbling into the camp of Midian, and it came to the tent and struck it so that it fell, and turned it upside down so that the tent lay flat." His friend replied this is nothing less than the sword of Gideon the son of Joash, a man of Israel: God has given Midian and all the camp into his hand.

Not only did these Midianites see their own demise in a dream from God, but Pharoah also had a dream that was from God and Joseph gave the interpretation. Pilate's wife was warned about Jesus. We also know that Abimelech had a dream, he was warned not to touch Sarah.

But God came to Abimelech in a dream one night and said to him, "You are as good as dead because of the woman you have taken; she is a married woman." Genesis 20:3

So we know that unbelievers can have dreams from God. However unbelievers cannot be prophets. Just because a person has dreams, this does not make them a prophet. A prophet of God will be recognized because he/she hears from God in dreams and visions. Prophets will have one or the other or both.

You may dream often. It still doesn't mean you are a prophet. It is just the way God is speaking to you in this season. However prophetic dreams are from God. You don't have to be a prophet to have a prophetic dream.

The closer we draw to God, the easier it will be to discern whether a dream is from God or not. If you are not sure, you should ask the Lord to keep the dream in your remembrance if it's from Him and give you the interpretation of it. Also ask the Lord what you should do with the dream. Sometimes the dream is a prompt to pray. Other times, the Lord will release you to share your dream with the person He is sending the message to. It is possible to have a dream but not receive the interpretation for years down the road. You can be assured, it will come at the right time. Another important thing to note about dreams. If a dream is from the Lord and you wake up and have a totally different dream the same night. Those dreams are likely to be connected. That dream is usually regarding the same subject. In Genesis 41, Pharaoh dreamed two dreams in the same night. One was about cows, the other was about grain. Both dreams pointed to the same message. God is speaking to you a message that He wants you to get.

You can have a dream about one person and the dream have nothing to do with that person. But the subject can represent someone else. Sometimes you may see one person's face but have a sense that it is someone else. Or call someone you know by a completely different name. This makes it a little more complicated to discern the meaning. We must be in God's face to understand His message. I have had a dream like this, and the message was for two different people.

Prophetic dreams require patience. We have to wait on God. The more symbolic a dream is the more we need to wait before sharing it with anyone. However there are times when you will have to share a dream without understanding it. Sometimes the message is just for the receiver. Maturity will tell us when to share and when to keep it sealed in prayer.

Those of us who are seasoned understand that you cannot share every dream that you have with every person you dream about. If you have a dream that someone died in your dream. The dream is prompting you to pray. If you were to share that with the person, they might be consumed with fear. God does not come to scare us. That dream may not even be literal. We ought to pray about every dream/vision that we have. We want to handle the messages of God with reverence and wisdom.

7

MUSIC AND THE MINSTREL

The soul of man, his will, mind, intellect and emotions, is tremendously affected by music. When something is difficult to memorize, we set it to music, because of its subliminal power.

Subliminal according to Webster's definition is 'relating to things that influence your mind in a way that you do not notice'. Commercial jingles are a great example of the subliminal power of music. I can remember jingles to commercials from 20-40 years ago. Hearing commercials over and over between programs or movies on television are effective ways to get us to buy products. If we read the ingredients on a generic product and they are the same as the name brand product, we will sometimes still purchase the name brand version. Talk about influence. Take a minute and think of a particular television program you like. You would probably have to admit that you like the show's theme song as well and it wouldn't be surprising if you knew every word. The power of music over our mind is nothing short of amazing.

Music is said to be a universal language. Major music stars are known to travel and perform their songs in countries where they can't even speak the language. Yet, their music sales skyrocket and their songs remain at the top of the charts in that foreign country. Even if you are not a lover or fan of music overall, it would be pretty difficult to deny its benefit in the world and effect over society. Musicians, trained or self-taught, tend to hold special places in the hearts of people. Loud cymbals, quiet violins, heavy bases, high pitched guitars, melodic pianos, jazzy horns, the list goes

on and on. To my knowledge there isn't a country or people who don't have some form of music in their culture. It is so intertwined in all that we do and who we are that I couldn't imagine a day or lifetime without it. Let's use our imaginations and picture waking up one morning and hearing a news report that a bill was being proposed in Congress on the complete ban of all music in America. Now that would be the start of a civil war, that would lead to a world war involving everybody. The power of music in any society is so broad and invaluable it cannot truly be comprehended, just embraced.

On any given Sunday morning or afternoon, in the average church, there is usually a musical sound to escort the congregation into a place of worship or praise. It doesn't really matter if the songs are being ministered a-cappella or accompanied by instruments, there will be a sound. In the church, musical selections are many times shared before the message to prepare the hearts of the people to receive. Music is equally relevant in the marketplace as it is in the church. Stores play music because of its positive effects on shoppers. We sometimes find ourselves in elevators with music playing to help you relax on the ride up or down, especially if you have a hang-up with enclosed places.

Music riles you up or calms you down. Music helps to heal the emotions, the mind, the heart, and even promotes healing in the body. We use music in the church and in society to such a large degree that it's worth looking into its value to the prophetic atmosphere.

In the book of I Kings 18:41, we read, "And Elijah said unto Ahab, Get thee up, eat and drink; for there is a sound of abundance of rain." Elijah spoke these words to the king of Israel, Ahab, under Jehovah's directive. Three years prior Jehovah God had instructed Elijah to inform this same king that there would be no dew or rain in the land. (I Kings 17:1). After the three years were up on heavens calendar, Elijah was told by God to go show himself to the king and that He would release the rain. This is such an extraordinary passage of scripture with so much packed inside for the prophetic people of God. We look here and see the prophet interacting with God, with the king, with a governor, with the people of Israel, and with the false prophets. In reading the whole chapter, you will see that after overcoming every obstacle Elijah was still able to hear. Hearing is a key and essential element of the prophetic calling and office. We place a lot of value, rightly so, on the seeing of a prophet, but in this chapter, I must call your attention to the hearing of the prophet.

Elijah could have simply said it will rain and waited for the visual manifestation. For our benefit, I believe Father God had the writer write "…for there is a sound…". Music is relevant to the prophet because it is a sound, as we will discuss a little later. One definition of sound is, 'vibrations that travel through the air or another medium and can be heard when they reach a person or animal's ear'. Well let's understand that this prophet could hear before he could see. He heard vibrations traveling through the air, that reached his ear. He was clearly able to distinguish that these vibrations were the sound of rain. In this recording of events, it is not recorded that anyone else heard this sound. This prophet was so confident, he sent his servant back seven times (the number of completion) until the servant could see with his own eyes the cloud, shaped like a hand, that carried the rain that Elijah heard coming. I told you this was an extraordinary passage of scripture. A hearing ear is a necessity to the prophet of God. Let us remind ourselves of what was written in Jeremiah 23:21 about the false prophets, "I have not sent these prophets, yet they ran: I have not spoken to them, yet they prophesied." True prophets speak what God speaks, and only when He speaks. We as prophetic people must keep our ears to heaven like the prophet Elijah and hear only the sound Father sends traveling through the air.

We know and all agree that music is a sound, and one definition of music found is 'vocal or instrumental sounds (or both) combined in such a way as to produce beauty of form, harmony, and expression of emotion'. Now please understand that music does not create a prophetic word; it helps carry a prophetic word. Ephesians 2:1-2 says "And you hath he quickened, who were dead in trespasses and sins; Wherein in time past ye walked according to the course of this world, according to the prince of the power of the air, the spirit that now worketh in the children of disobedience:" As we stated earlier, sounds are vibrations traveling through the air until it reaches the ears of a person. A prophetic word can be spoken without music, but with the music the journey may have less obstacles.

We must remember that all true prophetic words began with our Father which art in heaven. Prophetic words that begin any other place are false words spoken by false prophets. In saying that, let me say that a false word does not necessarily mean the messenger is a false prophet. Sometimes novice prophets developing their listening ear or distracted prophets can improperly relay a message that can be construed by some as a false word. If this takes place, I can assure you that the messenger will be ministered to by Holy Spirit quickly. If that happens the best recourse is to repent to Father and ask Him to clear the air.

Now back to the prince of the power of the air, Satan. He influences the realm of the second heavens and the earth itself. He cannot run anything in the third heavens, but his influence in the air and the earth is real. That is why we as Spirit-filled believers have been given authority over all his works no matter what atmosphere he is in. When words are released from heaven there are demonic forces that come to hinder those words from reaching their place of divine destination. Prophetic words must travel through the air and battle demonic forces every time they are released. The target in the battle is the hearing ear of the prophet and the heart of the person receiving the word. Our enemy understands the strategies of warfare very well. Destroying communication between two allies or joined forces is one of the best strategies in any military strike. If military troops cannot communicate with each other, they have no real chance of victory over their enemy. In every major war, there was always an attempt to destroy communication systems. Wires, bridges, bunkers, radios, airplanes, pigeons, coded readings, spies; they were all targets of destruction because they were sources of communication between military officers and soldiers. We, as the soldiers of the Lord, must recognize these tactics of the enemy, and always seek to protect and keep open our lines of communication.

Music from the heavens being played by a minstrel while a word is being released is very important and beneficial to the release and reception of that word. When that word is being escorted by music from a minstrel, it is the same as the President or any other high official being escorted by the CIA, Navy Seal, and Army Special Forces to his place of destination. Let's remember that music does not create a word, it carries the word. It is that prophetic sound that makes the transition from heaven to earth smoother. It is a gift to the prophet, not a requirement. This gift is in operation because of Holy Spirit. Whether it's one, two or two thousand people in a room, the language of music can bring everyone on one accord that the will of God can be accomplished.

The importance of music and sound for a prophet makes the position of a minstrel essential to the calling and office of the prophet. All musicians are not minstrels, but all minstrels are musicians. They should be skilled, anointed and set apart for His service. Playing a few cords to stir an atmosphere does not qualify one to be a minstrel. Living a holy life, walking in the Word, and staying in the presence of God are absolute necessities for a minstrel. The word of God released from heaven is always pure and holy.

Therefore if one is to call himself a minstrel, he must realize he is escorting something precious from the heavens to the earth. Minstrels who play for the glory of God, are prophetic people playing prophetic music for a prophetic move of God.

In II Kings 3:15, we see Elisha call for the minstrel to play as the hand of the LORD came to rest on him for the word of the LORD to be released. In this passage, Elisha went from a place of agitation to a place where he could release God's word accurately and righteously because of the minstrel. Setting an atmosphere by release of a holy sound is a sacred place for minstrels to operate in and should never be taken lightly. We must remember that no flesh can glory in His presence. In order to release a holy and anointed sound, minstrels should stand, walk, and live in a place of holiness and righteousness in Christ. Many times, I've witnessed minstrels attempting to come into His presence, without being in His Spirit, hoping the gift will suffice. We must understand that the Holy Spirit is in control and even if the minstrel is off, Holy Spirit will flow through the yielded prophetic vessel. Yet, we must also accept that the consequences of disrespecting the presence of God are still grave. Let us as prophetic people love Him enough to serve Him out of a pure heart and a holy life.

In another passage of scripture, we see young David play as a minstrel for King Saul, as he was often troubled by an evil spirit. In reading I Samuel 16:21-23, 18:10, 19:9, we see the soothing power of music from the minstrel. We also take note that for a positive outcome a yielded vessel is still required. Music played by a minstrel such as David is designed to shift the atmosphere. It is not for show or entertainment, it is to activate the presence of God.

Finally, I must mention I Samuel 10th chapter that also speaks of Saul, before he was anointed king. In this passage, he was in search of some family property, and that search led him to the prophet Samuel. While with Samuel he received the word of the Lord that he had been chosen by God to be the king of Israel. Samuel accurately ministers the word of the Lord to Saul without being accompanied by a minstrel. He also prophesied to him that on his return home he would meet a company of prophets accompanied by minstrels. This encounter with the prophets and minstrels became a place and time of prophetic activation and kingly ordination for Saul.

As prophetic people we must understand that before there is ever a change, there is always a sound. The enemy of our soul already understands this. With that knowledge he always seeks to pervert or distort that sound. He can only be successful when there is a lack of submission and holiness. We understand that minstrels must open themselves to the spirit realm in order to hear heaven. This yielding to the spiritual atmosphere can also be an open door to attacks from the enemy.

Let me elaborate. Musicians are passionate people. Open to emotions, feelings, and thoughts on a level that only a few can reach. They are attacked frequently in the area of lust. The same passion that drives them, if breached at the wrong moment, can open them up to lust and perversion on very high levels as well. That is why in the world, so many musicians are active drug users, fornicators or adulterers. All are arenas of perversion of passion. When musicians and minstrels exit the safety zone of accountability and submission, the enemy hits them with his best shot. This hit can be fatal.

Music and its effects are universal. Music is activated in a spiritual realm, whether the person is a Christian or not. It is so imperative that Christian musicians and minstrels stay in His presence, submitted to

Holy Spirit and accountable to spiritual authority. Musicians and minstrels operate in a spirit realm that a gift can get them to but can't protect them in. Traveling excessively, separated from spouses, family, spiritual overseers is not always wisdom. Timing is essential to the prophet and the minstrel.

Lack of intimacy with Holy Spirit through time in His presence and His Word is a sure passage to self-destruction for prophets and minstrels alike. We pray for the prophet, but many times fail to remember the minstrel. Hearing the sound of heaven and affecting a prophetic atmosphere for His Glory and His Word to be revealed is serious business. In contaminating the minstrel, there is a plan to distort the sound.

In distorting the sound there is the strategy to hinder the move of God. In the company of prophets, lives and yielded hearts can be forever changed. With that being said, may we as God's prophetic instruments in the earth seek to always bring glory to His name; living a life pleasing to Him, by being vessels fit for the master's use.

I know that all prophetic people are not created equal, so please read the next few sentences with an open heart. Prophets and minstrels are to keep their hearts and hands clean. If I keep my heart clean it means I am keeping my hands clean, as well. I want to encourage young prophets, seasoned prophets and minstrels alike to keep a watch over their eye gates and ear gates. Being used by Father God in the prophetic is a place of honor, restriction and surrender. This is not for you or I to be lifted up in our hearts, but for us to be bowed down before our King. Paul the Apostle said it best in Ephesians 4:1,

"I the prisoner of the Lord, beseech you that you walk worthy of the vocation wherewithal ye are called".

My sisters and brothers, my co-laborers in Christ, may I encourage you to stay close to His throne, that you may experience all that He has for you in this life and in that to come.

8

THE FALSE PROPHET: ROGUES, CHARLATANS, & WITCHES

⁓⧭⁓

"For there shall arise false Christs, and false prophets, and shall shew great signs and wonders; insomuch that, if it were possible, they shall deceive the very elect" Matthew 24:24.

The culture of this world is obsessed with the supernatural and spectacular. We are intrigued by it and drawn to it. And where there is a demand, the supply will follow. So there are false prophets popping up everywhere. We see them on reality television, social media, and basically everywhere we look. And just as the scripture says, they are so believable that if it were possible, the elect would be fooled. Thanks be to God, that it is NOT possible for those that belong to God to be deceived.

The false prophet comes in many packages: fortune tellers, psychics, sorcerers, astrologers, mediums, wizards, charmers, witches, etc.

These are both men and women who operate in a spirit of divination. They call on the dead and work spells which the scripture strictly prohibits.

Deuteronomy 18:10-13 reads

"Let no one be found among you who sacrifices their son or daughter in the fire, who practices divination or sorcery, interprets omens, engages in witchcraft, or casts spells, or who is a medium or spiritist or who consults the dead. Anyone who does these things is detestable to the LORD; because of these same detestable practices the LORD your God will drive out those nations before you. You must be blameless before the LORD your God."

Divination is any practice not specifically ordained in scripture that seeks to gain secret spiritual knowledge through another god. It is forbidden by God because it unlocks the door to the world of the demonic. It is a system of fraud. All forms of divination is sin.

Witches, psychics, and the like are quite dangerous. But the most dangerous of them all is the false prophet who claims to come in the name of the Lord. He is the most deceitful and cunning. The others come in the names of their own false gods. And so they are easily recognizable. But the covert deceiver is deadly. And while he or she may not be able to ultimately deceive the children of God, it is possible for them to do some emotional, or spiritual damage along the way. Weapons are formed against us even though they cannot prosper in the end. We will draw some attacks from the evil one. He doesn't stop seeking to turn our hearts away from the Lover of our Souls. Satan throws at us every scheme, plot, and fiery dart in his arsenal, hoping something will work to draw us away from God. He sends the prophet who has a heart like his. These are the charlatans and rogues.

"Watch out for false prophets. They come to you in sheep's clothing, but inwardly they are ferocious wolves. By their fruit you will recognize them. Do people pick grapes from thorn bushes, or figs from thistles? Likewise, every good tree bears good fruit, but a bad tree bears bad fruit. A good tree cannot bear bad fruit, and a bad tree cannot bear good fruit. Every tree that does not bear good fruit is cast down and thrown into the fire. Thus, by their fruit you will recognize them." St. Matthew 7:15-20

A false prophet disguises himself or behaves himself as if he were a committed believer. However inside his character is twisted. He is something other than what he pretends to be.

A false prophet lacks character

When a person's lifestyle doesn't match his witness, he lacks character. According to definition, a charlatan is a person who falsely pretends to know something in order to deceive others. Some definitions say, con artist. So a false prophet is a spiritual con artist. He must pretend to be more than he is in order to draw people to himself. He lives one way in front of people and another way behind the scenes.

"And hereby we do know that we know Him, if we keep His Commandments. He that saith, I know Him, and keepeth not His Commandments, is a liar, and the Truth is not in Him" (1John 2:3-4)

John calls him a flat-out liar in this verse. A false prophet does not keep God's commands. They are people who are living in unrighteousness (fornication, adultery, homosexuality, hatred, etc.) yet want others to see them as holy. If they can get you to see them as God's agent then you will come to them for a word from God. But how can God give them words for others and not speak to the sin in their own lives? This is inconsistent with the character of a Holy God. He directly tells us we shall know them by their fruit.

Charlatans also prophesy information that they have gathered from other sources. They talk to those close to you and pump them for information. Sometimes they stand back and observe you and are able to deduce information that way. Either way, the information is not given by the Holy Spirit. Therefore it is NOT truly prophetic.

There are many who profess to be prophets who are indeed NOT. They are pretending to be more than they are so that people will like, respect or admire them. Some are seeking power. Others do it for money. None of these are the right motivations.

A false prophet is obsessed with money

The word rogue has two definitions that we want to use in referring to the false prophet. The first one is a dishonest person. The false prophet who seeks after filthy lucre lacks honesty. He is looking to increase his pockets at the expense of the people. They are coerced, tricked or coerced into giving. His job is to shake the person free from his money *by any means necessary*. He will use whatever gimmick available. Some have been told to give a $1000 offering to get a house from God.

Give a $100 offering to get a spouse. None of these methods are Biblical. And all the money goes to the false prophet with the best tricks. And you never receive the things you were promised. As a result, people get angry with God for the evil of Satan.

God asks us to give but out of a cheerful heart. We are never to give out of guilt or anger; nor to buy a blessing. We sow into His kingdom freely out of love. If we study God's Word, it's hard for us to fall for the smoke and mirrors. Follow those who follow God.

A false prophet cannot be corrected.

The second definition of a rogue is one who is no longer obedient or controllable. He or she is a renegade. These are the false prophets who do not submit to leadership. They are not accountable to anyone. Many times they do not belong to a church. They just run rampant over the country looking for speaking engagements. No one can correct them or speak into their lives. This rogue prophet promotes himself as one who *always* speaks the oracles of God. Therefore according to him, he is never wrong.

While they submit to no one, they attempt to control others with their "prophetic words or dreams". Some of these rogue prophets pretend to submit. But upon closer examination, they speak ill of their leader and rebel against instruction.

A false prophecy

The false prophet wants you to turn away from truth to follow a lie. So they will tell you precisely what you want to hear. They give comfort in vain (Zechariah 10:2). They will prophesy things to lure you away from where you've been spiritually. They will prophesy many of the longings of your heart. That's why it is important to delight ourselves in the Lord. We need to have the right desires, only wanting what God wants for us.

As believers, we are to wear all 'material things' as a loose garment. Hold tight to nothing, but our faith in God. Because if we should hold anything too dear to our hearts, the enemy is able to set us up for the fall. He will entice us with the thing that we want most. The safest position is to want nothing more than a close relationship with the Righteous One.

A false prophet can perform signs & wonders

False prophets can actually demonstrate with signs and wonders that come to pass. If we are people who walk by sight, we will be easily fooled. We shouldn't be so naive to think that Satan has no power. He can produce miracles. So it shouldn't surprise us when a false prophet can produce a sign. Signs are for the visual. We are warned to walk by faith. This will keep us from being so enamored with the spectacular.

Many will say to me on that day, "Lord, Lord, did we not prophesy in your name and in your name drive out demons and in your name perform many miracles?" Then I will tell them plainly, 'I never knew you. Away from me, you evildoers!" St. Matthew 7:22-23 NIV.

"Suppose there are prophets among you or those who dream dreams about the future, and they promise you signs or miracles, and the predicted signs or miracles occur. If they then say, 'Come, let us worship other gods'—gods you have not known before— do not listen to them." Deuteronomy 13: 1-4 NLT

A false prophet can give a true word.

Don't assume that the false prophet always prophesies a false word. This is not true. A false prophet can prophesy or speak truth. In the book of Acts, we see a prime example of this:

One day as we were going down to the place of prayer, we met a slave girl who had a spirit that enabled her to tell the future. She earned a lot of money for her masters by telling fortunes. She followed Paul and the rest of us, shouting,

"These men are servants of the Most High God, and they have come to tell you how to be saved." [18] This went on day after day until Paul got so exasperated that he turned and said to the demon within her, "I command you in the name of Jesus Christ to come out of her." And instantly it left her." Acts: 16:16-18 NLT

What the young woman was saying about Paul and company was true. They were servants of the Most High God and their mission was to tell people how to be saved. Her words were true. Her spirit was wrong. Paul didn't need an evil spirit to announce his coming. It's not so much what a person is saying that makes them a false prophet. It's the spirit by which they operate. *True prophets are directed by the Holy Spirit. False prophets are directed by other spirits.*

A false prophet is into self-promotion

Another characteristic of the false prophet is that he/she promotes him/herself. Years ago, there was a televangelist that announced to the television audience, "Look how I healed this man!" We know Jesus as our Healer. Perhaps the man was healed through his ministry, but he did not acknowledge Jesus Christ, through which he was able to access the healing. He took all of the glory for himself. This man was indeed a false prophet. God will share his glory with no man. We do not heal in and of our own strength, but it is by His spirit that healing is activated.

A false prophet also seeks after speaking opportunities. He/She may even tell a leader that God told them to speak at their church. God is able to open the doors that He wants opened. We should never seek to prove ourselves to others or promote our own ministries.

Be wary of those who promote themselves. True prophets seek a heart of humility. They understand the danger of glory-seeking. It can cause you to be disinherited.

"I have come in my Father's name, and you do not accept me, but if someone else comes in his own name, you will accept him" (John 5:43).

It is very possible for a true prophet to start out right but become a false prophet. The falseness of a gift or office points to the character of that person. It is not measured in only the accuracy of a word given.

9

THE SPIRIT OF JEZEBEL

There are now numerous writings about that spirit, however, there can never be too much teaching about an enemy that destroys with such cunningness as the spirit of Jezebel. This may be your first reading on this spirit called Jezebel, if so please read with a prayerful heart. It will enlighten you. You may be that Christian who has heard about it in a sermon and are in need of more understanding. This is that more. Maybe you are a senior pastor or leader in the church, this chapter is definitely written with you in heart. Wherever this writing finds you, I hope at the end of this chapter that you are glad you kept reading.

The Bible says in Proverb 4:7 that "Wisdom is the principal thing; therefore get wisdom: and with all thy getting get an understanding."

Let's begin our journey with a very real truth, there is no woman named Jezebel running around the church chasing after believers. Jezebel is a demonic spirit in the earth released from hell to destroy leaders and believers in the body of Christ, it is a spirit. Whether a pastor, apostle, evangelist, administrator, teacher, usher, prophet or deacon, Jezebel is sent to destroy. She searches for a host to operate through, therefore you can find her anywhere using any open vessel. As we briefly review her history and her current status in the church, we hope that you will know her traits, recognize her through behavior patterns, and be able to cancel her works without fail.

Understand that the spirit of Jezebel may be operative in a male or female. Years ago, leaders and teachers in the body of Christ led believers to think that wearing makeup and being a seductress were clear traits and signs of a woman yielded to a spirit of Jezebel. With further learning and revelation by the Holy Spirit, it has become clear and acceptable that those where erroneous teachings due to prejudice and a lack of study. Today, we have excellent teachings on this subject that makes warfare more effective and deliverance for those under her influence more attainable.

The Bible records Paul admonishing his son in the faith, Timothy, to study to show himself a workman that need not be ashamed, II Timothy 3:15. Due to the shallowness of this teaching in our church history, many souls have been abused and ministries overtaken due to the workings of this cunning and deceitful spirit.

This spirit is referred to in female gender as Jezebel because that is the gender, and the name used as it came on the scene during the days of Elijah the prophet (I Kings 16 - II Kings 9). In her history, she was a controlling, greedy, manipulative murderess being led by Satan to bring Israel and its prophets to their knees. John 10:10 states that the thief (the devil) seeks to kill, steal and destroy, that describes the spirit of Jezebel accurately. It is that spirit that prophets warn you of and some leaders never see coming. It is cunning, strategic, intelligent, creative, patient and has excellent leadership ability.

The spirit of Jezebel has an assignment to destroy by any means necessary. It operates well around ambitious overachievers as well as compassionate generous leaders. Her range of destruction is so wide that you cannot always pinpoint her target even as the best spiritual sniper in the Kingdom. This spirit is never to be taken lightly. I have seen one too many leaders who believe they can outmaneuver this enemy and have failed. One thing that our enemy in the spirit world has over the church is the ability to respect time. Satan, knowing his end, has no issue waiting for his time to strike and he does that well while sitting or serving in the church. Even though Hollywood has exposed the tactics and ugliness of war in the world and the spirit realm, believers have yet to believe it is real. We bury our head in the sand and cover our eyes from the truth that stands in front of us daily.

We do this just to hold on to our dream world belief system that all is always well in Zion. I am a witness and victim to that spirit working right next to you undetected and busy as a bee. I also believe some of this oversight is due to the desire to see the good only and deny the possibility that such a spirit can use the one closest and most helpful in our lives. I will repeat what a pastor once said to me years ago, 'If Jesus had twelve disciples and one of them was used by the devil, who do we think we are?' That wisdom opened my eyes, but not wide enough.

Jesus' team of twelve was put in place by Father God himself, John 17:12 says, "While I was with them in the world, I kept them in thy name: those that thou gavest me I have kept, and none of them is lost, but the son of perdition; that the scripture might be fulfilled."

In Jesus' knowledge that Judas would betray him, He stayed ahead of the game. He walked out His purpose understanding that an enemy was in his camp. He totally surrendered to His death on the cross initiated by the treasurer of His own ministry team. It was part of the plan from heaven. Judas' betrayal was never an attack undetected by Jesus. If he had exposed Judas harshly or too soon, it would have negatively affected destiny and the hearts of those around him. Sometimes our enemy is so intertwined with our destiny and ministry that we must allow him to stay in place until an appointed time. Leaders have information that others are not always privy to, and sometimes have to refrain from reacting and even over-reacting due to personal pain from the knowledge we possess. Even if a spirit of Jezebel is operating in your ministry or church, dealing with it quickly and harshly may not be the best recourse. Just like our Savior, we should always stay in sync with Father's timing. That doesn't mean that we are yielding to the enemy, it simply means we are strategists like our Father in heaven. He always has a plan and it always ends in victory if we seek His face and stay in His presence.

Prophets in God's army are called to rally and lead troops into battle, expecting nothing less than victory. We seek His face, hear His voice, choose to follow His instructions without compromise, and learn to trust His decisions in all things. This may sound like the way the entire body of Christ should be, but for a prophet it is an absolute necessity to master. True prophetic people have one agenda, to do the Father's will. When we deviate from that for selfish gain or personal agendas, the Kingdom suffers violence unnecessarily. One thing that prophets and prophetic people must understand is that we are God's voices in the earth. What differentiates a false prophet from a true prophet is not just what we say, but why and when we say it.

We speak when He speaks and for no other reason except He is speaking. Many people want the prophet to share a word at their whim which may not be in God's will. We want what we want, when we want it and expect all of heaven to yield to that. That mindset is what surely opens the door to a Jezebel spirit to operate and nations to fall. Nations are not only large groups of people on a continent, nations are also the individuals of a group of people.

Jezebel spirits operate with and through the spirit of a false prophet so closely it is difficult to detect her presence, because they are not detecting the false prophet. This spirit is well known for positioning itself in high places of influence and always gravitates towards leaders as a key part of its overall agenda. Jesus quoted Zachariah 13:7 in Matthew 26:31 when He said, "...All ye shall be offended because of me this night: for it is written, I will smite the shepherd, and the sheep of the flock shall be scattered abroad." Cutting off the head (the leader) is a warfare strategy that has been used without fail to destroy ministries and churches for ages. The apostles and prophets are the foundation of the church, as stated in Ephesians 2:20. Therefore if I want to destroy a ministry or church, just like any building, all I need to do is set my explosive devises in and around the foundation which houses the infrastructure of that building. When I hit the detonator, the explosives at the base of the infrastructure cause everything to come crumbling down without fail. This strategy works in the home as well. Take a brief glance at the structure of the family where Father God has set the man as the head, the leader. Satan has strategically caused the families demise by influencing men to leave their wives and children, leaving them without a foundation or protection. The man leaving the family or not fulfilling his role in the family is like setting off explosive charges at the foundation of a building. Therefore the God ordained structure of family can be destroyed, allowing Satan to recreate an infrastructure totally against the blueprint that Father God ordained in the earth. In view of that, we must remember this, our God is sovereign, and He always has a plan of victory.

In taking a look at this strategy we understand why it is so important that the spirit of Jezebel needs to align herself with leadership wherever she is in order to accomplish her mission of destruction. Those who operate under the influence of this spirit usually have good leadership skills and are very creative. These traits must be there in order for them to rise to places of influence within the church kingdom. They pride themselves on being able to come into the church and get close to those in authority through their ability to fill gaps and solve problems. We take note how those under the influence make themselves available and necessary to a leader's agenda. They do it so well that a leader has to wonder how they could 'ever do without them' These traits of a Jezebel spirit are so close to those of a true prophet, that true prophets must consistently examine themselves and stay under divine authority and accountability to stay clear of this ungodly influence. False humility is not the answer, true submission from a clean heart with clear motives is.

Historically, Jezebel was a Phoenician princess, daughter of King Ethbaal. The Phoenician region included many cities, but the two most well-known are Tyre and Sidon. They were a prosperous people of trade, building and creative in manufacturing and development. They are said by most historians to be the creators of purple dye and they also created the alphabet system. Phoenicia is also known by the name Canaan, the land that Israel conquered to inherit their promise from God. Imagine the pride of this Phoenician daughter, with such a prestigious history, coming to Israel and becoming wife to the King. This unholy alliance was planned by their fathers. I am sure with the greed and wickedness of both bloodlines, there was not one objection at that wedding ceremony.

In her marriage to Ahab, seventh King of Israel, they created the most powerful political alliance of the ninth century. It was the first and worst of its kind, and was never to be repeated in Israel's history. Ahab, husband to Jezebel, became king of Israel during a time when the chosen people of Israel were under two separate governmental rules. One rule was the southern kingdom of Judah made up of two tribes, Judah and Benjamin. The other was the northern kingdom of Israel made up of the remaining ten of the twelve tribes of Israel.

Unfortunately, the northern kingdom of Israel was well known for their reign of wicked kings, but none were worse than King Ahab who followed in the footsteps of his father. I Kings 16:30 reads, "And Ahab the son of Omri did evil in the sight of the LORD above all that were before him." He was recorded to be worse than all the kings who preceded him, and if that was not enough he had the audacity to marry Jezebel, a princess of a heathen king and priest. Ahab, following Jezebel and not Jehovah, took his wickedness even further by building a place of worship for her false god Baal in Israel's capital city of Samaria. Samaria was the seat of leadership and political power. Ahab and Jezebel insisted it also become the place of spiritual degradation for Israel. This king was not only wicked, but he was also foolishly courageous as long as he had Jezebel by his side.

In understanding the spirit of Jezebel, we need to understand history. As we can see from just a brief look back, this spirit seeks power and influence. In order to attain this power it will go to great lengths, even murder. Time is not of the essence due to the spirit of Jezebel's overall plan. It is never in a hurry and is always about the ultimate goal of positioning. While waiting for its time to rule, it can and will wait you out, while sitting in silence, which is easily mistaken as meekness. All the while, it is behind your back, tearing down your name and character, so that those who once honored you will come to doubt you. Getting the faithful to take a second look is her key power play. Those who love you, serve in the kingdom beside you and have walked with you in ministry, will easily begin to question and doubt you because of the influence of this spirit. The Jezebel spirit has one main goal, to attain power. It will do it through you and then without you. In order to rise to a place of power this spirit must take a leader's place after becoming a key influence in the leader's life and ministry. In order to take my place, you must eliminate me, that is spiritual murder. Most leaders promote those with this spirit to places of leadership because they seem to deserve to be there. The only problem is that along the way, we ignore the urges to second guess our decisions and go back and inquire again. It all makes sense spiritually and naturally, and it looks good on paper.

They are available, intelligent, helpful, skilled, creative and have the seed to meet the need. Just like Jezebel. The alliance of her nation to Israel was what was needed to accomplish the goals Ahab, and his father had set in place. The deceiving part about this connection is that most leaders are not attempting to be greedy or rule un-righteously. Leaders are only seeking to do the will of God and are always grateful for the assistance to do so. This is such an innocent heart and motive, but a sure door to the spirit of Jezebel. We sometimes forget to watch as well as pray. We pray for help and when it comes we are so grateful, we stop watching and just keep doing. In that atmosphere is where this spirit rises to power. It is a strategist and knows that we, His chosen leaders, are sometimes caught up in the work and forget about the war. In that place is where it moves into position to divide and conquer, while we are hard at work for the Master. In all of this what shall we say about cancelling the assignment of this wicked spirit in our lives and ministry, and moving forward with the work and warfare. Let me say this first, those under this influence can be delivered, but it is their choice and begins with acknowledgment and repentance. Being used by this spirit is not the end all. Our God is a God of deliverance and a loving Father.

Romans 10:13 cites, "For whosever shall call upon the name of the Lord shall be saved." We can also reference King David after committing the sin of adultery and murder, Psalm 51:10-12 reads, 'Create in me a clean heart, O God; and renew a right spirit within me. Cast me not away from thy presence; and take not thy Holy Spirit from me. Restore unto me the joy of thy salvation; and uphold me with thy free spirit."

"If you call on Him, He is faithful and just to forgive" I John 1:9.

There is hope for those who seem hopeless, but true repentance, deliverance and wisdom must prevail. The spirit of Jezebel is a spirit that through spiritual warfare and prayer can be evicted from the premises of any leader, ministry and church. It seeks to control and manipulate those around it, but with exposure to the light it has to surrender. It must be confronted. Denial and fear are hiding places for any spirit. Therefore it is imperative that spiritual leaders open their eyes and hearts to the nudges of the Holy Spirit, no matter how unbelievable the thoughts may be.

Jezebel received her authority to operate in Israel from Ahab, through that unholy alliance. In aligning with Ahab, she strategically positioned herself before the people as a person of influence and validated by the king. Therefore she was seen as an authority in Israel and was able to send the country into poverty, and its prophets into hiding. The spirit of Jezebel has to be delegated authority to operate. Therefore, we must always locate the spirit of Ahab before we can cancel her works. Sometimes it's a husband, sometimes a father, and sometimes a spiritual leader, male or female. Leaders serve and lead out of pure hearts and are never to be blamed for the rule of this wicked spirit. It needs authority to rule, and through manipulation cloaked in false humility and service, it deceives the most anointed leaders in the kingdom. As leaders in ministry we must remember that once we give a person a position, title or a microphone, they are now individuals validated by leadership to influence God's people.

With this validation their sphere of influence increases and so does the need for more spiritual check points in their lives.

Senior leaders are called to feed the sheep and guard the flock, and we must do so with all diligence at all times. When we receive help in fulfilling that assignment we must continue to watch as well as pray.

That includes watching and praying for those who help oversee the flock. People under the influence of a Jezebel spirit got there by being enticed and driven by a desire for position and power. Sometimes they come into the church with this type of lust already in their hearts. And sometimes they are seduced after too much praise and too much influence. In old fashion terms, they 'get the big head' and the enemy slips in.

Have we ever noticed how some servants with the least recognition stay faithful and untouched by Jezebel. We don't shout their name, give them flowers, or even stand them before audiences to show our appreciation. They quietly serve and do their job for the glory of God. That is not to say they don't deserve it, or it is not good to give honor to whom honor is due. It is to say we must not allow the spotlight to be so bright that it becomes blinding. We must not aide in the servant losing his or her focus. Watch those who are close and pray for them often. Teamwork, unity, humility and accountability will help every ministry and leader stay clear of the influence of the spirit of Jezebel.

What does one do if this spirit rears its ugly head in the ministry, church or in one's life? Answer: cut it off. The answer is simple, the process is detailed. To 'cut it off' means to take every ounce of influence and delegated authority it has been given. You must do it in love and wisdom. Always praying for the deliverance of the host, hoping they may shake themselves from the snare of the evil one. Releasing those operating in this spirit from places of authority or influence should be done inch by inch, step by step. That way you can unravel them from their connections and victims with little to no permanent damage.

Telling someone that another person has a Jezebel spirit and that they need to back away is not always best. Outside of teaching, wisdom and timing, it can do great damage. It may also cause that spirit to draw sympathy and support it doesn't deserve. Some will feel you are misunderstanding them, harshly judging them, or better yet, you are just jealous of them. We must also remember they have been planting explosives devices all around you or your ministry for some time now.

In any warfare, there must be a plan of strategy in disarming and removing harmful devices. That definitely is true in the Kingdom of God. Let me suggest a warfare plan that may help you. First, I encourage you to diligently seek God, because every warfare is different, and territorial spirits have to be considered. Then gather your loyal intercessors, you won't be able to gather them all because that spirit is probably on the intercessory prayer team. Next, move forward by teaching on the subject so that those in the church or ministry can have the knowledge to recognize the enemy, no more hiding. Soul ties have been formed and alliances created with this spirit so move cautiously, but not fearfully. We must remember, they were placing explosive devices all around the ministry, and until you locate them all you must walk carefully. Moving abruptly or too quickly can be dangerous to innocent hearts and the ministry overall. The Holy Spirit will quickly began to alert you to things that were hidden every step of the way. You will hear and see things differently because you are more alert on the actual battlefield.

Let's visualize how bomb disposal technicians operate as they locate and disarm one or more explosive devises. They are confident because they have been trained and have knowledge equal to or above that of the one who set the device. They have on all the proper armor and have all the necessary gear and tools to get the job done. They go in because they have been trained to save lives and this is what they do. There is nothing personal about disarming a bomb, it's all business. Before the assignment they were somewhere safe from all harm. They came because of a call. They came to do their job. That is the way leaders must move in ministry. We must trust that we have been called, chosen, equipped and prepared for the work. We go in wisely, confidently and strategically because that's what we do. We allow God to use us to save lives.

God has not given us a spirit of fear. The Jezebel spirit is just that, a spirit. This is not a special spirit; it is just another spirit. The Bible says that we have been given power and authority over all the works of the enemy and nothing shall by any means hurt us. Luke 10:19

We must not allow this or any spirit to intimidate us and cause us to run from battle.

We need not back down from this fight or any fight..

We have been trained for this.

Our trust is in Christ, our Chief Commanding Officer.

The Bible says in II Timothy 2:3-4 that we are to endure hardness, as good soldiers of Jesus Christ, not entangling ourselves with the affairs of this life; that we may please him who has chosen us to be soldiers.

Let's follow Him into victory as He saves many souls alive.

The war has already been won.

10

HOW THEN SHALL WE PROPHESY?

‎━━━◆◆◆◆◆━━━

We prophesy by the measure of faith that we are given. However we cannot hold faith as the only virtue by which we prophesy. If we do, we will find ourselves prophesying without the Holy Spirit.

We don't get to prophesy whenever we feel like it to whomever we want. Just because someone wants a word, doesn't mean we can give it. We just can't make it up as we go and call it faith. It is imperative that we prophesy by the spirit of God. That requires patience. We have to wait on God. And sometimes God is silent on purpose. Jumping ahead of him will cause us to be in error.

Of course the more time we spend with God, the more precisely we can hear from Him. But our seek must be authentic. We don't spend time with him just to get a prophetic word. God created us for relationship. We are summoned to intimacy. Our relationship takes priority over the working of gifts. Gifts should flow out of a pure love relationship with the Lord; not as a replacement.

To prophesy by faith, all other elements must be in place because faith only works by love (Galatians 5:6b). In the past, we have seen angry, bitter prophets spewing words and even curses at God's people. Wounding people in Jesus' name is a serious infraction. It does not go unnoticed by a Holy God. That's why it is necessary that we spend time in God's presence examining our own hearts. St. Matthew 7:2-5 says we are hypocrites if we do not.

"For in the same way you judge others, you will be judged, and with the measure you use, it will be measured to you. "Why do you look at the speck of sawdust in your brother's eye and pay no attention to the plank in your own eye? How can you say to your brother, 'Let me take the speck out of your eye, when all the time there is a plank in your own eye? You hypocrite, first take the plank out of your own eye, and then you will see clearly to remove the speck from your brother's eye"s.

We must take care not to wound God's people.. However know this: those who operate in the prophetic will certainly find cause to be offended. People will reject you, avoid you, despise you, talk about, be jealous of you and misunderstand you. However maturity will cover your heart from taking it so personally. The words you prophesy are God's; therefore the rejection is of Him first. If they reject Him, who are we? We will receive the same treatment that He has. Nevertheless, no matter what offense comes, we can never allow it to settle in our hearts. Offense stinks. It will fester and cause our hearts to become bitter, and callous.

"A good man out of the good treasure of his heart brings forth good; and an evil man out of the evil treasure of his heart brings forth evil. For out of the abundance of the heart his mouth speaks." St. Luke 6:45 NKJV.

So in order to speak on God's behalf, we must guard our hearts with all diligence maintaining love at its core. Love must be our pure motivation.

If I have the gift of prophecy and can fathom all mysteries and all knowledge, and if I have a faith that can move mountains, **but do not have love, I am nothing.** I Corinthians 13:2

Loving through offense is God's picture of how the prophetic should work. We taint the prophetic any other way:

➢ Refusing to give someone a word because you are angry at them.

➢ Only prophesying in anger about areas that you know a person has a struggle.

➢ Hold back a part of a prophecy because you feel the person doesn't deserve it.

➢ Mistreating someone because of offense.

➢ Prophesying a chastisement because of the way you were treated

➢ Telling others about the offender

The Apostle Paul warns against misusing spiritual gifts in a loveless way. We absolutely must prophesy from a heart of love. If we have any part of unforgiveness or bitterness in our heart, we position ourselves to abort God's purpose. We will taint the word that God gives. So we must work to keep our hearts pure. Or you can find yourself in serious trouble with our Loving Lord. We are to choose to love even when it's hard. He expects us to say what He says, nothing added, and nothing taken away. Leave all avenging up to the Lord.

Most people don't mean to harm others. It's just that their flesh gets in the way. Sometimes the cause is plain old immaturity. Like the 3-year-old who tells the lady on the bus that she stinks, they don't understand the harm that they do. We have to allow people room to grow. That means offense will come. But throw it off and keep on moving.

Even if your anger is only directed at a different offender and not the person to whom you are prophesying, God still takes issue with it. Your heart has pollutants in it and you are offering it to someone else. If you have an issue to work through, do not continue to prophesy over the clutter of your heart. Take time to deal with your own issues. It is unbalanced to hear God for others but not hear Him for yourself.

We must continually make a decision to love. The Word tells us when there is an offence, to leave our sacrifice at the altar and be reconciled to our brother. *Relationships take priority over gifts.*

Love the difficult. Forgive the mean. Pray for those that are hateful. It is the command of our Kind King. We are forgiven and so it is incumbent upon us to forgive all others. It is the way of salvation. Love demonstrated is the best prophetic expression a person can ever minister. We show the way of God. For our God is love. Every prophetic person must prophesy not just out of faith; but out of love.

So how does one get there from here? There is only one path. That is
the path of humility – the low road. We must be intentional about
pursuing a humble heart. The primary understanding must be that
God's prophetic message is to draw men and women into relationship
with Himself. It's not about me being right. It's not about how I look
to others. Nor is about me knowing anything. It is quite the contrary.
Christ is everything and I am nothing. As John the Baptist stated, He
must increase and I must decrease.

"For what we preach is not ourselves, but Jesus Christ as Lord, and
ourselves as your servants for Jesus' sake." I Corinthians 4:5.

We cannot stake a claim on the praise of men. All praise, honor, and
glory belongs to our God.

The prophetic is an amazing ministry. Because is flows out of the
supernatural, people are often astonished at the accuracy of a prophet.
It is like no other ministry. While all of the gifts are challenged with
the praise that they draw, the prophetic is very delicate. It yields an
abundant harvest of praise and glory far above its counterparts. This
is the caveat. We must be on guard that we don't become intoxicated
by the accolades.

None can prophesy of his own accord. We are dependent on an
omniscient God. He knows and reveals to those he chooses. He
whispers his secret into our spirit. It is foolish of us to take glory for
what clearly belongs to Him. Christ must always be exalted.

Those who prophesy are not better than others. We have no power on
our own. We don't get to prophesy because we are holier, wiser, or
more obedient. In spite of how the crowd makes us feel, We are not

to be seduced by the aroma of the applause. We are to fan it all toward Heaven, understanding we have no power disconnected from Him.

"For who makes you different from anyone else? What do you have that you did not receive? And if you did receive it, why do you boast as though you did not?" I Corinthians 4:7 NIV

If any of us need humility, he will stumble into humiliation. Unless we humble ourselves, we will find ourselves humbled. As the scripture reminds us, pride surely comes before a fall.

When Christ is diminished and the prophet is elevated, we have certainly lost our way. Our call is to exalt our God and not ourselves; preaching Christ and His Kingdom. Humility's motivation is to simply love Jesus and obey His commands. Nothing else.

So if we will prophesy, let us not prophesy just out of faith, but out of our love for God and with an humble heart.

ABOUT THE AUTHORS

Prophetess Torrona Tillman is the seventh of eight children, and a native of Chicago, Illinois. She is honored to be the blessed wife and best friend of Larry Tillman for over 26 years. They currently reside in Northwest Indiana with their two adult children. Alongside her husband, Apostle Larry, she oversees New Destiny Ministries and conducts leadership seminars and conferences. She operates as a five-fold ministry prophet to the body of Christ and ministers at churches, women's conferences, seminars and workshops for His Glory. She is known and honored for her wisdom, her passion and her servant's heart. To God Be All Glory Forever and Ever.

Prophetess Crystal is the love of Apostle Oscar Jones. The couple joyfully celebrate nearly 35 years of marriage. Crystal is the loving mother of 7 adult children 2 of which are bonus children (in-laws) and the beaming grandmother of 8 little darlings. Prophetess Crystal serves as prophet, conference speaker, mentor, and author. She has ministered all over the country and abroad. She has been the featured guest on many radio and television programs, CTN Live! and Atlanta Live! She has authored and co-authored about 18 books. She lives with her husband in the Atlanta, GA area.